I0170300

# Letters & Sounds

## Books by İlhan Berk in English Translation

*A Leaf About To Fall: Selected Poems*, translated by George Messo
*Madrigals*, translated by George Messo
*Selected Poems by İlhan Berk*, translated by Önder Otçu
*The Book of Things*, translated by George Messo

# Letters & Sounds

~ *Poems* ~

# İlhan Berk
*Translated by George Messo*

R·H·B

This English edition published 2014 by Red Hand Books

RED HAND BOOKS
Old Bath Road, London SL3 0NS
1618 Yishan Road, Minhang District, 201103 Shanghai
150th Avenue, Springfield Gardens, 11413 New York
Serifali Mahallesi, Umraniye 34775 İstanbul
Cross Road A, Andheri, 400093 Mumbai

**www.rhbks.com**

ISBN: 978-0-9575977-3-0

Copyright © The Estate of İlhan Berk, 2014
Translation © George Messo, 2014
Introduction © George Messo, 2009, 2014

*Yesterday I wasn't at Home, I Took to the Hills* was first published in the Turkish original as *Dün Dağlarda Dolaştım Evde Yoktum* and published by Adam Yayınları, Istanbul, in 1993. This translation follows the edition published by Yapı Kredi Yayınları in *Akşama Doğru* (Vol. III of Berk's Collected Poems), 1999. All remaining poems are taken from İlhan Berk's *Toplu Şiirler*, published by Yapı Kredi Yayınları, March 2003.

Four translations from Part I appeared in earlier versions in İlhan Berk's *A Leaf about to Fall: Selected Poems* (Salt, 2006). Other translations first appeared in *The American Reader, Shearsman Magazine, Bülent, Shadow Train* and *The Argotist*. The introductory essay, 'Berk-like: Prisoners of the Word', first appeared in *Turkish Book Review*.

*All rights reserved. No part of this book may be reproduced or transmitted in any form or by any means, electronic or mechanical, including photocopying, recording or by any information storage and retrieval system, without permission in writing from the publisher.*

*This book is sold subject to the condition that it shall not, by way of trade or otherwise, be lent, re-sold, hired out, or otherwise circulated without the publisher's prior consent in any form of binding or cover other than that in which it is published and without a similar condition including this condition being imposed on the subsequent purchaser.*

Printed and bound in the United Kingdom.

# CONTENTS

Bel Canto

# Berk-like: Prisoners of the Word

~

Ambivalence, contradiction, ambiguity all lay at the heart of İlhan Berk's poetic credo. *Writing is a kind of hell,* he once wrote. And again, *I'm a prisoner of the word, big time.* And yet, if his work alone is a measure, Berk's is a 'hell' of compulsion rather than confinement, his 'prison', — the visionary lexis of his poems — one of seemingly endless range.

Few poets have been so consistently pioneering, so restlessly innovative:

> *One of the ways for a poet to go beyond his contemporaries is to incorporate new languages into his work; but that's not enough, he also needs a new technique. This is how we come to notice a poet in the first place: If he is unconventional. A new language and a new technique are the starting points.*

*Every poem,* he says, *is the beginning of an adventure.* And the genesis, the point of ignition may take us anywhere, as in his poem 'İstanbul.' What starts firmly in the empirical facts of a picture's details — a small black and white engraving by Braun-Hogenberger — soon encompasses the whole of Pera, Galata, The Golden Horn. By slow degrees, the poem weaves its verbal labyrinths. Part travelogue, part stream of consciousness, the effect is dazzling and, as the poem itself declares, 'Berk-like.'

To be inside a Berk poem is to experience the kind of disorientation familiar to us from a hall of mirrors. Recognizable detail blurs, is obscured, shaped into new perspectives and suddenly rides into intense focus as we move from room to room, mirror to mirror. Or in this case, from line to line, from poem to poem. The surreal, the disembodied, invite us to reengage with a world more sensual, more erotically charged for having been misplaced, as here in the poem 'Black Amber':

*Your mouth is the boy selling dark blue birds in the market*
*It's a three-monthly magazine called Field*

*Our small rivers are your mouth*
*Coming down a narrow street each day into a small square...*

Berk resists the kind of cerebral posturing we've come to expect of late modernist experimental verse. Invariably, it is the sensual mantra of the felt world that sparks his imagination and propels the poem's inner logic: a taste, a smell, the texture of something touched, a word overheard, a glimpse among trees. Berk calls out for us to re-enact the poetic moment through shared experiences of the world as sensory object. To know is to have sensed. To know the poem is to open oneself to it physically as the reawakening of a softened sensation.

There is, in Berk, that perennial allusion to passage, from one place to another, from one state to another, through levels of awakening and consciousness, sightings and reappraisals. The journey of those co-existent yet inanimate objects that share our daily lives forms the poetic thrust of his great long work, *The Book of Things*. Berk's poetic alchemy transforms and transports the over-looked, the neglected, the everyday, elevating substance and form to the realm of anima. Mud has a soul. So does trash. Rooms and doors and windows feel *us*, as much as we feel *them*:

*I want to make one more contribution to my reputation as a man of small subjects. I want to add dust, mud, rubbish, stone, dot, dash, question mark and slug. I want to bring the trilogy of* Ev *(House),* Çok Yaşasın Sayılar *(Long Live Numbers) and*

Birşey Olanlarla Birşey Olmayanlar *(Things That Count and Things That Don't) together under the name of* The Book of Things.

Slowly, we are coming to know İlhan Berk. In 2006 *A Leaf about to Fall: Selected Poems* introduced him for the first time to a British audience. It was followed two years later by *Madrigals.* November 2009 saw the release of *İkinci Yeni: The Turkish Avant-Garde,* a pioneering anthology situating Berk in a broader cultural and experimental poetic context. And then, in 2009, his monumental poetic trilogy, *The Book of Things,* translated in its entirety, confirmed a growing reputation in the English speaking world. Now we have *Letters & Sounds,* a multi-voiced selection of some of the poet's finest love poems, elegies and lyric prose. Berk is fast becoming one of the best known Turkish poets in Britain. A small but significant library of his work is to hand; we can read him at length, — broadly, variously — and not before time.

*George Messo*

# PART I

Yesterday I wasn't at Home, I Took to the Hills

(14 EKİM 89)

.15/nnlm(7.1.92

▬▬▬ ▬▬▬

▬▬▬

② DÜN DAĞLARD DOLAŞTIM EVDE
YOK-
TUM

'gerçeğin yapısını dilin yapısı be-
lirler.! (wittgenstein)'

⑤

I

*"poeta pirata est"*

# OKTAY RIFAT

Of "a sea that is no visitor."

A child like everyone else. He loved desert landscapes, fish (which he knew even in childhood slept without closing their eyes), herbs, mountain goats, girls on bicycles.

In vast summers he played in front of their homes. He collected butterflies, oyster shells, marbles.

With his youthful beard no matter how many crazy birds there were he could imitate them all in a single breath.

An Alchemist.

If his hand touched a tree, it was suddenly even more a tree.

His name was fished from the aqueduct at Ephesus.

He felt the voices of beloveds in their handwriting.

As a lawyer he sought motives for crimes in Homer, Hammer, Bedreddin*.

His poems he wrote in opposition to the gravity of language. And that's why images there speak in his name.

---

* *Bedreddin:* Sheikh Bedreddin (1359-1420), theologian and preacher who led a rebellion against the Ottoman Empire in 1416. GM.

The terrible child of poetry.

He had the stamp collector's fetish, but for words. (Long before us he found that the limits of language are the limits of the world.)

So it was he began to use the world as his home.

One of three handsome men. A Prince.

His bed in the subconscious was always spread.

Tall, with a black moustache. He had a beautiful youth like Leonardo da Vinci's. He wore good clothes, spoke well.

His hair was always unkempt, no one touched it. (So it was for birds to comb it.)

In his youth he was one of the Istanbul surrealists. But he went everywhere with a leaf from Niğde*.

---

* *Niğde:* A small city and rural province in Southern Central Anatolia. GM.

As experienced as a bottomless lake. (Assignations, vagrancies, pastoral poems, nights like the puff of a cigarette, talk aimed straight at the sea…)

All of it, all for living and to die for.

A Renaissance man. Was it he who said "Poeta pirata est"?

A historical grey.

The poetry?

A book of citizenship.

*Exordium*

In 1988 his death was about its work, welcomed him at its door. He assumed the manner we know.

Did he say: "My words are done, now I can darken my path"?

So it was. The life of the world passed in an instant, and he saw it!

That day, did you ever look out on the sky over Üsküdar?*

---

II

# YESTERDAY I WASN'T AT HOME, I TOOK TO THE HILLS

The sun fathers a cloud in my pocket. I wrote: the stone is blind. Death has no future. Things have only names. And: "A name is a home." (Who was it said that?) Yesterday I wasn't at home, I took to the hills. A gorge looked at us, what it said still lingers in my mind. It was this: we sensed infinity within it. Objects are held in time. The tailors' lamplighter Hermusul Heramise's goatskin rose to its feet every spring. Rain cannot not rain. Stone, not fall.

What was I saying, the world has no thoughts. Grasses don't get bored. A pencil thinks it is a tree. The horizon, a hoopoe. I don't know about you, the world is here to be mythologized. It has, therefore, no other end. Transforming into a myth, to be a myth! That's what we call eternity.

Wherever I start, that's where I return. So I'm going. I have work to do on that grand statement, death.

# THERE HAVE BEEN TREES I HAVE MADE FRIENDS WITH

"I filled silence with names." Codified things. I have known the sky's and the trees' infancy. There have been trees I have made friends with. There still are. I didn't understand the Milky Way. Nor numbers. (They behaved as if they had yet to be discovered.) Except for eight (5+3) with whom I became intimate friends. (Who hasn't?) A little with zero too. (It's not been so easy to find zero.) I've heard terrible things about three. Why? I don't know. To know is a number. And I've also met one. You can't think with one. Some numbers are born guilty. One of them is one. I loved stones without asking why. The relation between the pebble's name and its shape has not been proved. I couldn't find a thing on the history of black amber. Fine. Mystery is everything. There are some consonants I couldn't read. (The letter's spirit abounds in consonants. American Indians knew this well.) I accompanied birds. Except for the turtledove, birds know nothing of numbers. Horses, I understood, don't dream in the East. (In Homer horses weep.) I have seen mountains while walking. And thinking as they walked. Recognition impedes reason. The World is ours! Said the snails, talking among themselves. I can't say I understand that. Nor that I don't understand it. One should read snails.

VIII) (Harmonia.) (105)

AĞLAYARAK ARKADAŞLARIM OLDU

(BİR sözcük yolunu.)

Sen ırmaklardan yüz çevirirken buluşuyor ırmaklar, otlar gözlerinde bir izdüşümüdür
(bir yerlere yüz bularak) zamanın ortasına çıktığımız
... İsa'nın hayaleti hâlâ dünyanın üzerinde dolaşıyor. Gerçeği yansıtmıyor sözcükler buna göre değil. Türün dışında pencereler olmadığını biliyoruz. Ölüme inanmam bundan. Yaşam yolunu öldürmüşün, ben sadece sorularımı sormak için yazdım İnsan. Zamanı bilmiyoruz. Zamanın yüzü yoktur çünkü. Yalnız adı vardır; yüz her şeydir; duvarcılarım avuçlarında taş bunun için ölür durur. Taşın yüzü bulununca, taş adını aldı. Ben senin ırmaklarla buluşuruz — Hevine dönmek istiyorum. Sonra da... sonra diye bir şey yoktur. Toprağıdır... Sonra,

Sözcüklerin biçimi yansıttığı yere su götürür.

Türün dışarıya pencereleri durmadığı doğru değildir.

As you talk about rivers the rivers themselves are talking, grasses are in their eyes. Time is an illusion. Write this down somewhere. It's not true that spirit has no outward facing view. Jesus' ghost still roams the earth. (I only ask. It's only to question that one writes.) Those who forget their youth stagger in the morning. The rose exists because it is named. Stone got its name when its face was found. (Which is why masons turn stones around and around in their hands.)

I want to return to your eyes. And then... There's no such thing as "then." "Then" is outside history.

# LETTERS AND SOUNDS

Shihabüddin Fazlullah* spoke with thirty two letters and did not have a soul. He believed in letters and earned a living knitting skull caps. It is said he saw every letter in the human face. In the Zeyl he wrote to Cavidan (which hasn't been found), he assigned the letter A to sky; to water: C (water is from Thales); to death: U (Death is a bit U). To fire: Z.

The world was the letter, all forms. Sophocles, who, like Pythagoras, did not know how to draw, was also of the letter, as was the cricket, and Mohammed too.

---

* *Shihabüddin Fazlullah:* Syrian scholar and writer, 1301-1349. GM.

Mohammed (whom we know, spoke with twenty eight letters and had a soul and no bird could ever have flown to where he did) gave ear to sounds. He listened only to them. Everything was sound. Heaven and Hell were sound. A peacock was sound. If Tu Fu* rode to Rice Pudding Mountain to graze his horse, it was sound. Which is why he always felt a void between the soul and the forms. And why he seldom wrote. Why should he? Language is lonely. It doesn't speak. The universe is more talkative than us, he said. More leaf-filled. The sun speaks with images. A tree works noisily. So does a stone. Night descends in noise. The universe is sound.

"The alphabet is a peddler."

* *Tu Fu:* One of the greatest Chinese poets of the T'ang Dynasty, 712-770. GM.

## WHICHEVER ANGLE WE TAKE, EVERYTHING EXPLAINS ITSELF

Everything, everything began in the moon-watching city of Babel.

Names followed. Once named, everything became boring. The silence was broken. The enormous silence.

In history there are no animal names to be found, you say*. Nor the sounds of flowers' names… yet sound….is everywhere.

I don't forget that everything had it's place in the world. I saw that Time became unrecognizable once it acquired a name. A bird couldn't remember its name any-old-how. As for the mountains, not one of them knew its name.

Wonderful.

To name something is death!

---

* History, this phallus memory.

# HOMEROS HER SABAH YÜRÜRDÜ

# DÜŞÜNMEK İSTEMİYORUM

(27)

~~GÖZ İÇİN YENİ BİR ŞEY YOK~~

her gün

~~Gökyüzü s. kızarıyor~~. Her akşam güneş batıyor,
her sabahki Çinli kuşunu dolaştırıyor. Bir ağaç
bin yıl sonra inliyor. Bir yıl sonra her karınca.
Dünya bir ... Füzuli Kâdını 7'e benzetir-
di. Homeros her sabah güneş ... yürürdü.

*(heavily crossed-out draft lines — largely illegible)*

yalnız oldugum ...

Düşünmek istemiyorum ... Dünya benim

Bir akşam durup durulan dünya-
mın yuslanmasını gördüm ...

~~Görmek yordu beni.~~ Anlamak kocalttı.

Göz oldu. Tarihini ...

Göz'dün. Tarihini kapattı.

Göz için yeni bir şey yok.

Whichever angle we take, everything explains itself.

Mehmet the Conqueror was short.

Amos was a farmer of Pharaoh figs.

Al Farabi was swarthy.

If only we'd never known names. The world we see through names is not the world. That's why we go to our graves never having seen the earth. There's nothing without its own weight. We should have started from here. Mad Time was left outside. We were separated. Now whatever we write we write about death; death and time.

I don't know why but these days I read death vertically. Try it yourself. It's worth it.

I'm cutting it here. I hear a blade of grass talking as it does. I'll also be at the bird's birthday party. Night awaits me. We know the way.

# DÜŞÜNMEK - İSTEMİYORUM

Gökyüzü ~~sileses~~ Her akşam güneş batıyor.

*[heavily crossed-out lines, illegible]*

Her sabah Yediruda Homeros. ~~Bilmek istemiyorum.~~

Diyorsun, nesnenin sonu mudur? Öteki için
~~den~~ ~~Montaigne'i~~ söyler güneş. Sandalye ~~çınlıyor.~~

Ancak ~~görülen~~ transport şeyler. ~~Saymak~~ isteyormuş.

~~yeşilden~~ ~~Sessizlik~~ ~~Sophokles~~

~~resim yapmayı~~ Dünya sonra ~~yorma~~ isteyormuş.

Tin ~~kelimesi~~ Düşün-tür ~~durup~~ düşürken ~~kimseye~~

Göz için yeni bir şey yok.

*[crossed-out line]*

Görmek yordu beni.

Anlamak, ~~koca~~tır. ~~Bana gidiyorum.~~

*[illegible crossed-out line]*

# I DON'T WANT TO THINK

Nothing's as old as this world. The sky is sick. The sun is ordinary. The trees are unskilled. Every morning a Bedu goes to work on his camel. Every evening two Chinese walk their bird.

The world is a repetition. A tree looks a thousand years into the future. Sees a dinosaur a thousand years away. Ghazali* used to liken himself to the number 7. Homer used to walk every morning.

There is nothing new to the eye.

This is terrifying.

---

* *Ghazali:* Abu Hamid Al Ghazali (1058-1111), philosopher, theologian and mystic. GM.

**VII** (imge evi) (birbaşlarına) (duv bellekler)
karşı çıkarak —

onaltuğlaç kozları atlar, balıklar, ışınlarla dolaırken
— bu sınır taşları —

sözcükler sizim anısımızdaki yeşamlarını
yine süvdürürler. Dünyayı evleri bütün
yağmurlarıyla duvar/ar, dükkânları
kapatırlar, yatak tuşlarına ekarlar

Ben
dört bin yıl önce kalan oküllerin, gelinlerin, hal-
varlarımla Cudi dağında gemiyi karaya vuruy-
Nuh peygamberimiz tümcesine — anlamın kıyı-
ması dolma imgeleri süverler. ( imgeler,
yazmsel sözse duymaz, görmez )
Türlü kılıklara girip akarlar, sessi,
kokuya, zenge, sessizliğe dönüşürler (
konuşması beyazdır, sessizdir ünlü )
sözcük olduklarını unuturlar. ( Sözcükler imge
dönüştüklerinde tanınmaz ... nedeniu kırmızı
bir sözcüktü.) Bazıları eğreti imgelerin daya-
nılmaz büyüsüne kapılırlar dünya en eğ-
retilemedi ... adlarının son iki harfini atarlar
( sözcükler sık sık bunu
da simgelerin
silirler. Bir harfta arazi değildir.

Adlandırmak ölümdür.

başka yerli?

dan

buyruğunda

has vururlar

Was it Göethe who said "Time is my field"? I don't want to know. From where it sits a house overlooks Montevideo. The chair is urban. The window is feudal. Water ran without memory. The soul is alone. When I was a child I wanted to be a river. Rivers always called to me. I don't want to think. The world thinks for me instead.

The word is dead.

Bronze: Monarchic.

Iron: Democratic.

One evening I suddenly saw that the world had grown old. Seeing wore me out.

# IMITATIONS

In former times trees were an alphabet. All letters were trees. A, fir; C, nettle-berry; O, apple; M, cypress; P, olive.

Truth lies side by side with imitations. Nothing at all can escape it.

We found and knew the world thus.

"Trees are salmon!" I once heard an Eskimo cry from the place where he lay.

This world belongs to imitations!

With trees it's impossible to know what their letters think (trees laugh in the face of imitations). Trees just want to be trees, and letters, letters.

And we know with trees it's not a question of recognizing or knowing their letters. I've seen many a river, mountain, plain (Ibn Battuta could read plains) wandering around in disguise; it's enough just to be on the earth. We always forget that trees talk. In the past we didn't know how to forget. Time had not been divided. Past and future were one. Time was a transparent noun: Seen on looking.

The end of imitations is the end of the world.

We're all there, in it together.

# THE SIGN WASN'T YET THE NAME

Once, words had lives outside of ours, but no meanings.

In those days, a strop razor, a water bucket, a horse could live easily side by side.

In those days, we had no such intimacy. Our acquaintance with balcony is recent. (Balcony is our childhood.) Previously, red was a sound. Narcissus didn't know its name. It lived as it pleased. The word "death" used to have two syllables too, would go in and out of houses, stroll around beds, and ridicule trees. Just as today, it performed its task alone.

The sign wasn't yet the name.

Once, words never cared less about meaning. When the prophet Noah said "I am the prophet Noah who sat in the dark bowels of his ark on Mount Judi two thousand years ago with my wife, children, my brides and animals" the words – to rid themselves of meaning – let images loose (images the poets set down on paper every night of green Mohammeds and yellow Jesuses), words that forgot they were words. (Transformed into images, words are unrecognizable: Take away words, the world stops!) Sometimes bedazzled by analogies – analogies are the royal road to poetry – they would stamp out their names. All under the command of symbols (one who touches symbols can't be saved) driven here and there by the wind.

The sign wasn't yet the name.

# ASKELOPIS

Askelopis Ephesos'lu bir kış... dolaşır ve
bizim görmediğimizi görürdü. Nesneler ja-
... sever. Herkese görünmez şair gibi de-
... bir dille konuşur. Onu kimse kavrayamaz.

suyu ölmez,...
Ben orman öyle ... bir dana da ...

... sabah ... ne ...
bir ...

... Dildir ... Tek Kranik ayak basılma-
... sevgili dil.) Bundan nesnelerin öte-
şimdi bir şey yoktur. Görünmeyen üstünde
susmalı. Konuşmalı. Askelopis onu
görmedi. Ölüm' onu görür kılar (felsefe
bir de ölüm-ü öğrenmek değil midir?).

Nesneler yalnızlık mı diyorsun?
Nesneler bundan böyle yalnız diye duyar...
... yazar. Söz.

[*]

[*] Ey bellek, senden kurtulmuş yok!

# ASKELOPIS

Askelopis used to walk around with a bird from Ephesus and could see what we couldn't. Objects are like that; not everyone can see them. They love secrecy. Like poets, they too speak in a white language. Reason cannot grasp it. Yet there is nothing that is invisible. Objects don't know this. Why should they? After all, it's not for objects to know. Do fish know the water in which they swim? I recognized the forest without knowing it, and never forgot it*. There's no way of stopping them, once objects turn into words. They envelope the world, then turn into thousands of sentences. In some corner of the world, every morning, a thousand objects wake for this. I came to know the world through sentences. The outer limits of the universe. Language is the only god, that fetus!

(My beloved language, do not conceal those untrodden paths and keep me from seeing them.)

There's nothing more to objects than this. This much Askelopis could not see. Death revealed this to him. (Doesn't philosophy, after all, teach us something about death?)

Would you say objects are lonely?

From now on objects will never feel this kind of loneliness again.

I promise.

# WATER CLOCK

Eternity... Eternity...

There are no suitable words for eternity. There are words close to death. We associate with them in the world. When we are freed of the command of words – these death squads – objects too will enter the realm of immortality. Objects also yearn for immortality. When Imam Azam Ebu Hanife* met eternity, he wasn't at all surprised to find his earthly water clock right by his side. It was the first time a water clock had run outside time. He could hear it working.

Now that's a miracle!

---

\* *Imam Azam Ebu Hanife:* Abu Hanifah (699-767), Muslim jurist and theologian, and the founder of the Sunni Hanafi school of Islamic jurisprudence. GM.

14 Şubat 91

I 72

SUSARTI

sonsuzluk... sonsuzluk... Bozuk sonsuzluk!

WORDS ARE WORDS

45

Words kill the desire for eternity. They stick to death's agenda. Night's mouth is full of leaves, day's is full of night (night is a child), grasses' full of cloud. All day we carried inside us what we knew and talked of what we knew:

WORDS ARE WORDS

I have always confused words. Words always explain themselves. Sky speaks of its late-coming. Water speaks of horizontals. That words mirror the world is an idea that carries water. I looked at trees before kissing you. Did you see that the trees could see? That's how we talk, when we talk. Childhood flits from garden to garden. Death is what enters the narrative. Let's pass it by. The world has no idea it's turning. The spirit wanders blindly. Sun forgets its name when it sets.

# WORDS ARE WORDS

(82)

sonsuzluk... sonsuzluk
sonsuza gidel sözcük yoktur. Olsa yazılır
sözcük... Seylem sonsuz uzun alanına giver

Hacer el feytemi sonsuzluğa ...
dünyadaki susan...

WORDS ARE WORDS

sözcükleri ... Güneş ... telerinden söz eder
... Görüşten ayelek. Böyle konuşunca
Konuşunca. B... den önceye gelen çocuğun
Gerçeksizdir son/uşu anlatmaya çalışır
... oldugu yerde yoktur. Sözcükler
haber vermez. Tu habersiz dolaşır. Güneş
adını unutur batarken.

~

ölüdür anlatmalarına giren. Geçelim

# I FOUND THE ROCK WHILE THINKING

I found the rock while thinking.

I was coming back from talking with the grass. A dead leaf, a street that had forgotten its name, a statement loaded with allegations, a guilty river, a worn-out bird all walked with me. Life was a merry-go-round; we walked the walk.

I know nothing can attain the place words reach. The shirts of Jesus and Karahisari* were seamless. Words attest to it.

(O invisibility! Take my hand. At night the weight of words grows heavier. And... [A pity, I cannot finish my sentence.])

I always felt suspicious of meaning. There were houses, rooms I forgot them all. A world that knows nothing of its own existence. Trains pass across its face: it assumes itself.

---

* *Karahisari*: Ahmed Karahisari (1468-1556), a celebrated Ottoman master calligraphist. GM.

Everything, everything talks in the universe. Houses, children, rivers, geography. I read that rivers have no time.

Geography wasn't enamoured of its name. Meaning is boring. Three times a day it looks at itself in the mirror. It oozes loneliness. You can't make a house from meaning. I know, but my loneliness gets the better of me. I haven't any thoughts. A stone knows it's a stone, I don't. I destroyed my poem when I realized. From that day on I grew old like a river.

# III

*My face was small, tiny, so I thought.*
Turgut Uyar[*]

---

[*] *Turgut Uyar:* Poet (1927-1985). GM.

# BEAUTIFUL THISTLE

A face. Turgut Uyar. Beautiful thistle.

From Edirnekapı. And therefore a poor, hopeless street: Vaiz Street. Number 70.

Horse markets, garden cafés, camels and pale, green tramway cars: all for this indigent street.

A child, sensitive, frail. Even then he would say "I am trouble!"

Master Tanaş, his son Toma; the coal merchant Eda Hanım; and the lame grocer Halit. (This lame Halit goes every day to Karagümrük to have his hair trimmed.) The first faces.

So now his face is ready for a long journey. Cities big or small.

And Posof.

For poetry came down from the mountains into the village of Zanerhev. His jacket and stirrups are in the rain.

In a photograph in Posof he is stretching out to kiss his own face.

A pedestrian: "On the shore of all possibilities!"

A father, dignified, respectful. Always a horse, always mounted on a horse (that world walks hand in hand with this quiet, diligent father).

Was it Ankara that gave birth to this child? A bronze sky therefore.

His first question: "Does it ever rain in Mexico?"

His first book: Jules Verne.

His first cigarette: Hanımeli.

The first tree he saw: A nettle berry tree. (A knife in his hand skinning an onion.)

Sage-like, he unveiled the quantity of objects in nature, the weight of each.

His name, a whiteness. A shelter to himself. To his ash.

His words are the words of the womb. He always wavered between yes and no.

His language, the history of pain. A testimony, to his age.

So now you know why he drew death to his side whenever he sat, and why they stood together whenever he rose.

*Exordium*

One day when he turned off his lamp he said: "Poetry preserves nothing. It is opposed to everything."

And like a guilty sea he added: "Our heart will soon grow up!"

That's what he said and then withdrew.

Now his lamp, *Büyük Saat*\*, all the children know by heart.

---

\* *Büyük Saat*: The Great Clock Tower, Turkey's tallest clock tower, built in 1879, in the city of Adana, and the title of Turgut Uyar's *Collected Poems*, 1984. GM.

# PART II

# IS YOUR LOVE RED?

Is your love red?
    (Love, that wall-clock)
Once more I come to know
    Your love is red

Is your face night?
    (Your face, those tiny streams)
I've memorized all the colours
    Your face is night

Is your voice early evening?
    (Your voice, that shore)
I know, I've lived every voice
    Your voice is early evening

Are your eyes *Lake Hours*?[*]
    Your eyes are *The World's Most Beautiful Arabia*[†]
I've thought about every book title
    Your eyes are *Lake Hours*

---

[*] *Lake Hours:* Title of Ahmet Haşim's seminal poetry collection, *Göl Saatleri*, 1921. GM.
[†] *The World's Most Beautiful Arabia:* Title of Turgut Uyar's 1959 poetry collection, *Dünyanın En Güzel Arabistanı*. GM.

## IT WAS A LONG DAY I WAS RETURNING TO LOVE

It was a long day I was returning to love
Long, my one, as long as loving you
There I was, saying here is the first kiss your blue cleft
Here is morning's seven and your wet mouth
Here is some old grass of your groin and stomach
Here is what your tongue brought forth, here my forests
Here is your waking in the bed, stretching naked
Here striking rocks your old shadow your old voice
Here is that olive-skinned bird in your throat, that wild river
Stay like that, I said, stark naked, intimate
Stay like that, first I'll kiss you *there*
Dark as love is, it's a one-syllable word
Stay exactly like that my love, is what I said

## POEM

      Yellow, beautiful one, enters my city
Placing her lone and harem voice
She, like rivers, gently on my flesh.
Crimson, our mouths intertwine.
      We go through sky, a forest. Long
I sense them, your eyelashes. Wheat.
Your face is endless July, my suicide. These
Are your nether regions, Oh my Loveface,
                              Oh.

Love is a journey, and now that's you
To enlarge and increase our sexuality
To make mountains and skies of our nakedness.

I hold you this way to stream and sky.
Now I mix you wildly.

— A vast night reaches out from us now.

# THE SECRET HISTORY OF NATURE

I saw Nature's inner workings. Its movement and change
Like a History of people, of those born, living, dying
Scattering themselves
(putting forth their priorities and their discontinuities)

I saw running water renewing itself
I saw it inflamed, rebellious
rising.

I saw it and said: this river births me.

This flatness coalescing without the newborn or the evolving.

This pain impressing its form on salt and stone.

I saw that great arbiter, nature
I saw all that in nature is there for man.

# SKY DRIFTED OVER ME

I'm looking at sky coming and going
A stream runs beside me, over its stones
Then suddenly stops as if flowing no more.

I saw water changing shape and form
I saw it in the shape of my hand
I saw it had no form
In its vast history.

So it is I said, rising to leave. Sky dissolving
A horse flicked its tail, a goat stretched out
Step by step on stones I passed the running stream
Then watched the water I'd pelted with stones.

Sky drifted over me.

# SLOWLY QUIETLY I PASSED THROUGH CROWDS

Slowly quietly I passed through crowds
like the sea's surge swelling and ebbing
and slowly quietly I withdrew
within me from where it passed. Slowly
quietly I touched pain, quartz, poetry
slowly quietly weighed water, knew its weight
scents
geography.
Then leaning over I came to know the body, its order
and I saw the absolute flatness of silence
nothing that I saw did I see repeated
my exterior slowly quietly was made human
so I mingled with crowds
and like this I became a crowd.

# WORDS

I'm your mouth's words, your childish eyelashes
    (You, spring, flocks of birds)
Your panty lines
                        your darling pubic hair
And time (Time, that memory
in the body's history).
                  Then a faint memory
Of your naked flesh.


                          Love
    is wounded.
Wounded because all words
                  are those crusaders.
        (You, sunset, bell towers)
Look how I bring them one by one
                drop them into your mouth
All one by one every single word
            in your name
(as though touching you).

I that love, an "I" that is itself love
        (You, suns, vast skies)
Somewhere a snowdrop is breathing you now
                  Your panties slip
Your eyes, your enchanting, still nakedness.
            Love drops in your mouth.

# THE SKIN MY LOVE IS SLIPPERY

The skin my love is slippery
Like long, wild grass.
At night I touched your naked skin
My tongue roamed everywhere.

Over and over the knot of your mouth
Then I bent to your skin's hair
Our whiskey voice, voracious mouth, eyelashes
Falling onto my paper at night.


*The offer*

(Then I went out with your face
Into a street thinking itself a street
Out,
          as if it were late afternoon).

# THAT FLUID LOVE

Plural is beauty. Keep your face there
                (Your face, visage of a people's history)
Hold your mouth to my groin, sweet sin
                My body, that hell, in your body
                — My Sweet, let's make love.

It's dirty love, my child, that fluid fossil
                The womb, that exile, is everything
Think of the endlessly renewing stone
And remember the skin is history too
                Your mouth, that fire, in my mouth
                — My Sweet, let's make love.

# PERHAPS I TOO AM PROSE

Your face is a street leading down to the sea,
It's a crossroads, your face is a water clock

Whenever I bend down to your face
It's a market opening early

You are a lily without rhyme or metre
White I breathe upon you deep blue

As if I were working on a long poem
Your face conferred its longest rhymes

And who knows what your face rubs off
Perhaps I too am prose

# THE NAME OF PAIN

Slowly silently gold is gathered under your decree slowly silently
Slowly silently wheat is sown under your decree slowly silently
The people's bread is broken under your decree slowly silently.

With you silk darkens quickly rots quickly with you
Water quickly entwines turns turbid with you
The history of labour atrophies quickly with you.

And with you slowly slowly on copper quartz bronze slowly
Slowly written at length the name of pain appears.

# I AM PAIN

I am pain. I mean your sometimes abject face. Sometimes
Your neck bent in despair. Sometimes your mouth, your
                                        blackened eyes.

I mean your childhood. I mean a street in Bursa
(It seems to me as if I'd never seen Bursa)

Then the candle you lit one evening in a church
For a face that death had not yet come to know.

You are always turning into a face for me,
A face
That carries within it nights and dawns.

I am your ruin, the one you raised
In the written hand of pain.

# PART III

# PABLO PICASSO

*L'Homme au Mouton*
A light in the world, a lonely cloud, a lonely branch
Sky, a flower, water's terminal feeling, its love, yearning, happiness
A little hope, a little light a little further on morning
All individual, indivisible beauty, inseparately alone, together
Passing uselessly by.

Picasso embraced his brush.


*Nu au fauteuil noir*

A tree seen by windows
About to flower
Hands, hair, eyes of the armchair
Hands hair eyes by themselves
A woman looks at the sky
The woman, still, silent, just looking
Looking she says sky won't end with glances
The window says I'll not stand like this again

Neither blues nor blacks say look we will not stand like this again
In this world sometimes we expect what poets sometimes talk of
We'll stand like this say the hands
No one will try to move us from our place again
Hair says this is how I'll stay
First this happiness we see everything for the first time
Whatever is in the room, stone, mirror and everything else
        stands like this at the edge
It says.
Everything says something
Everything looks at something

Picasso looks only at them.


*Nature-morte*

Picasso woke
His olive-skinned hands.

# I WOKE IT MEANT A LOVE IN THIS WORLD
*(Rondo)*


I woke it meant a love in this world
— Your voice, like giving up on a rose.
I was black, like paper on all those lives.
You could see my name each day on seas
For a thousand years I was an M sound in Lower Egypt.

Wasn't it clear how I beat love
For a thousand years I opened you in loneliness
Whenever my name passed before your radiance
       It meant a love in this world.

Once, loneliness was beautiful in Egypt
It was a fresh clean sky that could be entered with you
Glancing, it blossomed like a lily in my memory
Now it's a shadow growing tall on my plains
So that's how I woke but not really awake
       It meant a love in this world.

# LOVE

With you here, we knew no evil
Unhappiness, misfortune were absent from life
Without you they lined up hope with darkness
Without you they crossed out our well-being
For days now the sea, seen through a window, is unlovely
For days now our humanity dimly lights through our absence
                                                    of you.

Come, take us to new times.

# BEL CANTO

## Prologue

The streets woke, strangely awake. Mussels were deep in sleep,
And the mouth of a child. The bonito, the porpoise, the lumpfish
And the catfish were awake. The black bream and the pink bream
Were asleep. Ilya Avgiri's cat took a look. Hristaki
Arcade was swimming with fish, a plate, a sleeping fork,
Koço's Christ-like face sleeping,

     What did Ilya Avgiri's cat do
     It opened a window
     All of Pera woke up.
     A girl sat up holding her breasts
A child laughed.
Avgiri raised all the shutters
Avgiri looked, fish everywhere
He set off around Karaköy.
Ilya Avgiri's cat observed the dawn
There was nothing else to do
He wandered off to Istiklal Street
Yawning yawning yawning.

## Chorus of Poor Mackerel

Where do they go, giving up on the world, these skies, oilman
                                        Boris Nihas,
        Nico the Knife Grinder
A window looking out onto a street, an old balcony, a newly
                                        knitted shawl
Ayia Efemiya, trout, Emperor Boao, the Polish Synagogue?
And what about Little Mason Street
Should the sky's sun rise and go
Ayios Ianios put the candles out, should he be dressed like us,
        and lost entering sky with two girls?
Nothing makes any sense no matter what.

## Chorus of Porpoises and Tuna

Hey, Saint-Michel, Dame de Sion, Robert College
We have eyes for no other's land.
We tuna, porpoises, poor mackerel
One Sunday we left the sea, bored
   Water, a window, a cloud
   A woman walking beside a flower
   Houses streets roads trees
   And houses streets roads trees
   Galatasaray, Little Duvarcı Street, Istiklal
   We, poor tuna, mackerel, porpoises.

Avgiri looked at the black bream tuna at all the fish,
the sardines, the pink bream
He saw them seeping through Beyoğlu.
Avgiri climbed Kızkulesi
Shouting shouting shouting
   (only Nico Margarit the Knife Grinder and Toridos
            the Tailor
and a gypsy flowergirl understood Ilya Avgiri's shouts.)

## Nico Margarit the Knife Grinder

You ask who I am
Strange, Nico the Knife Grinder
My job is to sharpen knives
Every clear cloudless Saturday evening
The oilman Boris Nihas, the prawn seller Ismail
A pesky child in and around Beyoğlu.
If clouds should break a window
I see it before anyone else.
If a woman undresses in a poem
I'm there standing in front of her.
My job is to sharpen knives
Against the sky all of God's days.

## The Gypsy Flower Girl

What happened to this Istanbul
Neither Sevim nor Yanula are here.
I really don't understand
The prawn selller just ups and leaves.

Sevim's window, the shah of windows,
Look at the state of it now.
It's pointless if you ask me
To look at the sea without Sevim.

Because it was enough for me
The sea, the laughter of a street.
Who can I sell these flowers to now
They've taken sun and moon and gone.
The cat stares, everything is in its place,
skies, tuna, prawns, Taksim Square.
(Avgiri woke his wife and told her of all
that had happened. Avgiri's wife was
sad she wasn't there. She went
and opened the window.)

## Lament of Ilya Avgiri's Wife

I passed my days at Soğanağa
A window, a palm-sized sky
Sevim Matilda Hayrünisa Eleni
To love a little more each of God's days
A little more the republic, more Ilya Avgiri

My youth was beautiful
Hand in hand with sea and wind
My beauty: select lines in every poem
Me, in the memory of each bed, in every house
Each day my story fragrant in mouths

Neither republic nor Avgiri concerned me
In the past I lived like an animal
A carnation between my two breasts
I used sky in place of a mirror
To look at my shameful places

No one in my youth no one bothered
With the moon, the republic, the sun
The sky and sea never left the world
But now fish leave water for the first time
In my time none of these things happened

# ABOUT THE AUTHOR

**İlhan Berk**, one of Turkey's most influential and innovative poets, was born in 1918 in the Aegean city of Manisa. He was the award-winning author of more than two dozen books of poetry, as well as volumes of critical and biographical prose. He was also an acclaimed visual artist. Berk lived for many years in the town of Bodrum where he died on 28 August, 2008. His books in English include *A Leaf About To Fall* (Salt, 2006), *Madrigals* (Shearsman, 2008), *The Book of Things* (Salt, 2009) and *İkinci Yeni: The Turkish Avant-Garde* (Shearsman, 2009), all translated by George Messo, and *Selected Poems by İlhan Berk* (Talisman, 2004), translated by Önder Otçu.

# ABOUT THE TRANSLATOR

**George Messo**'s most recent book of poems *Violades & Appledown* was published by Shearsman Books in 2012. His translation of Birhan Keskin's *& Silk & Love & Flame* appeared in the Visible Poets Series from Arc in 2013. He is the editor of the bilingual journal *Turkish Poetry Today*.

# A NOTE ON TURKISH SPELLING & PRONUNCIATION

With few exceptions, where Turkish appears in the book I have employed standard Turkish spelling. The exceptions are those words for which well established anglicized forms exist, such as İstanbul and İzmir, which are commonly written in English with I rather than İ.

As a guide to pronunciation the following may be useful:

a  (a in apple)
b  (same in English)
c  (like j in jam)
ç  (ch in chips)
d  (same in English)
e  (e in pet)
f  (same in English)
g  (g in gate)
ğ  (lengthens a preceding vowel)
h  (h in have)
ı  (i in cousin)
i  (i in it)
j  (like s in measure)
k  (k in king)
l  (l in list)

m  (same in English)
n  (same in English)
o  (o in the French Note)
ö  (same in German)
p  (same in English)
r  (r in rug)
s  (s in sit)
ş  (sh in ship)
t  (same in English)
u  (u in put)
ü  (same in German)
v  (same in English)
y  (y in yes)
z  (same in English)

www.rhbks.com

www.ingramcontent.com/pod-product-compliance
Lightning Source LLC
Chambersburg PA
CBHW031604040426
42452CB00006B/409